Vincent O´sullivan

The green window

Vincent O´sullivan

The green window

ISBN/EAN: 9783743308930

Manufactured in Europe, USA, Canada, Australia, Japa

Cover: Foto ©ninafisch / pixelio.de

Manufactured and distributed by brebook publishing software (www.brebook.com)

Vincent O´sullivan

The green window

THE GREEN WINDOW

THE GREEN WINDOW

BY

VINCENT O'SULLIVAN

LONDON
LEONARD SMITHERS AND CO
5 OLD BOND STREET W
1899

CHISWICK PRESS:—CHARLES WHITTINGHAM AND CO.
TOOKS COURT, CHANCERY LANE, LONDON.

PREFATORY NOTE

THE thing I call in this book *Will* appeared under a different title—*Le Scarabée Funèbre*—in the *Mercure de France*. It was put into French for that magazine by M. Henry-D. Davray; and I am glad to have a chance to say how much I admired his translation.

CONTENTS

	PAGE
I	1
FAINT	3
SOB	7
DEAR	9
SAME	13
THEN	17
WHITE	21
BE	23
VAH!	27
WEAR	31
CRAVE	35
WRITHE	43
GOOD	47
HELP	51
RUSH	55
SEED	59
YIELD	67
VAUNT	71
HAVE	75
BOW	79
WILL	83
OWE	95
GLIDE	99
SAID	103
WAS	107

THE GREEN WINDOW

I

SELF-DEVELOPMENT is the kernel of sagacity. Your main duty is towards yourself: you must be the bond-man of your own will. A whimpering baby, you come into the world as into an enemy's camp: you are not wanted there; henceforth the universe will be against you. You are in the posture of a new poet who is smartly told that the world would have been never the poorer had his effusions remained incoherent. "Here is "another pretender!" cries mankind, assembling against the latest comer. Remember you are not a volunteer, and it follows that you need not take a side. You are in nobody's debt. Your makers considered their pleasure; the country of your birth is a political accident, and is perhaps the first to hand you the mud; you had no choice about accepting the cup of life. The best thanks you can offer for existence is to make your days by fair means or desperate a matter of self-profit. Woe to him who stands in the way, whether as friend or open foe! You are to grasp your I firmly with both hands and use it as a bludgeon.

In this struggle things are not noble or base; they are merely expedient. Every man, however fair spoken, has in mind some secret advantage: he is for himself and therefore against you: you must cross Is with him. Your part is to have your I out of the scabbard before he can get his well in hand. Sweet words and actions are but brilliant parries; affection is a fatal snare; and you will be wise to regard all protests of sincerity with suspicion, since humanity tends to the vile. These are but tricks in the game, and the good player is he who is swift to use them for himself and to baffle them in others. Hold yourself in life as you would at a card-table where every one cheats. And above all, be sure to chaunt in your heart your own *Gloria*. That which you do you must think fine; what other people think does not matter in the least. Patriotism we are told (chiefly by interested persons) is a virtue to which we ought to sacrifice, and it is thought decorous to slave for the public fortune; but have you not perceived, that the man who is held most in honour by his country is the man who has been most successful in referring all to himself?

FAINT

FAINT

A LONG white road, powdered and heavy, with few trees to stand between it and a sun whose rays are javelins—such a road, and a mass of sweating and tortured pedestrians, is a fair picture of human life. Each of the walkers has started out to reach some nebulous point which he calls his goal. None can be without his goal: even he who stands aside indifferent and smiling makes it a goal to be indifferent. So with a goal in mind humanity marches. In the van a few walk with easy stride, dusted but a little, and scarcely panting; then comes the crowd of troubled hard-breathing adventurers, trampling down the bewildered ones who stand in the way and who, in their turn, make a third class as they lie, after the ruck has passed, groaning and wounded. Scattered amongst the mob are some who, while pretending to a cheery smile and sedulous forwardness, look askance at their boots and wonder if the game be worth the candle. These are the faint.

A swaggering attitude with hand on hip is not an invariable presentment of the swashbuckler, for

it

it is as often the mask of the faint. A scowl is the war-paint of the timid. It is very observable, that a harsh manner, and a mouth full of high words, veil the plaintive man. It is also observable that the faint one makes a virtue of the lack of action which his timidity compels. Thus, if he is hot for his friend's wife, and yet is too faint to address her, he will not seldom have such fine terms about honour and the chastity he loves, that folk must exclaim: "Lo, here is an anchorite!" when, in truth, the rogue is raging at his starched shirt. In this he is wise; if it be wisdom to twist our defects to advantage. Nor at times is a faint man without wisdom when he turns faint. I know of a thief who was one night engaged with his fellows to break into a house, but at the last moment he fell timid, and going to a parson said he would withdraw if he had the price of a "doss." He got the money and went honestly to bed; while his mates were every one of them laid by the heels. It is an art to know when to recede. Willow bends hopefully: "I stand," says *Quercus*, and is riddled by the lightning.

At twenty we see very near us Napoleon, if our ambition is to succeed, or Jésus Christ, if our ambition is to be good. At forty, Napoleon and Jesus Christ are very far off, yet neither has moved. Then we reel and are faint—too soon perhaps? For we may be nearer to them than we think—nay!
it

it is not impossible for them to take some steps towards us. And we may always hear the voice. A refrain sung by Syrens, out through the arches of the past it comes. . . . O holy song, O blessed singers, let me linger where the strong sound of you is as the tonic breath of the sons of God!

SOB

SOB

THE rain swirls, and my face is wet in the garden, as I wander there on this gray sodden afternoon. What heavy drops fall from the cypresses as they shake in the wind!—from the cypresses and the sad laburnums. I follow little gravelled alleys which run anywhere—everywhere, and meet at the wide road which is the middle of the garden. In this road are the marks of wheels: not heavy ploughed marks as of great and violent traffick, but the ordered decorous lines of solemn, unswerving—yea! relentless progression; and I am vaguely disturbed by the marks of wheels. On each side of the gravelled paths is the damp grass; and mounds are here and there with stones set upon them carven in the shapes of crosses or angels. On some of the mounds are placed white wax-like flowers, covered with globes of glass which are dimmed by the rain. A few thin women, clad in black, with yellow faces and haunted eyes, meet me from time to time. These are the mourners. In the distance, at the gate, a bell tolls: another funeral has entered. An old man leans on a spade,

and

and smiles at me as he points with his thumb to a square hole and a heap of clay. And still the rain swirls, and my face is wet in the garden.

I follow the main road to the crest of the hill; and now below me lies the city with its madding vices in its cloak of gray, and around me are the monuments, the splashing rain, the whining grass. Here too is a place where the earth has been lately stirred : it is without stone, without grass, a length of dismal clay. Have I been seeking this—is *this* the grave? It is the grave of my enemy—of my beautiful enemy whom I thought my friend, and mud seals the starry eyes.

The rain swirls—oh, the pitiless, never-ceasing rain, how it falls !—and my face is wet in the garden.

DEAR

DEAR

THE moment you love, you become a slave. For the thing that you love must influence and domineer: you are no longer in command of your forces. And to death, also, you make a humiliating concession, since you give it a means of torturing you beyond its due and ordinary power. So instead of being master of yourself, you become by loving the helot of two masters: Death, and the Thing you love. If you love your house, you are tormented when you are on a journey by the thought that it may be in flames; if you love your money, you are dreadful of wars, and famine, and riots, and the rise or fall of the stock-market; if you love a woman, you are afraid (if you be wise) that she will be unfaithful, or (if you be silly) that she will die. And in any case you are seized with a craven fear of dying yourself. Whatever it may be that you love, it becomes the black care that rides behind your saddle. So if you would be free, it were well to come early to the late conclusion of the soured King worn with pleasure, that every affection is vanity.

Hence,

Hence, friars and monks shew great wisdom in detaching themselves from earthly things; and that is why they are sometimes seen so cheerful and humane, and careless of death. I like the cold saying of St. Teresa who, when a postulant begged leave to send home for a book of Hours to which she was attached, replied: "Ah, if you are still "attached to something, you are out of place in my "convent." I knew a man who as soon as he perceived that he loved a thing inconveniently, straightway began to disfigure it: thus he would hold a binding close to the fire, or place a book face downward on the table, or hang a picture in a vile and harming light. So he weaned himself. I knew another who, when in the same case, would give away to some person at a distance the thing he prized, "For" (says he) "when I give it loosely "as though it were not precious to me, and cannot "get it back, I come to think, after a little, that it "has no value." This is the mortification that the friars use.

Sometimes love jumps with self-interest, and then it is sage to let it run, but not with an easy rein. In nuptial love it is expedient for the husband to be sweet with his wife if she be a sedulous guardian of his children; and the wife with her husband if he be not a man of mean parts, and make her life peaceful and joyous. It is wisdom in the conquering general to declare that he loves

his

his army: for most men are easily made drunk with soft words, and he depends upon his army. In the statesman too it is a mark of sagacity to say that he loves the people: for the people are his magistrate, and it is his business to propitiate the people. It has been laid down by some, that one should pretend to a love of one's enemy in order that he may be so drowzed as not to perceive what is working against him; but this is a well-handled ruse, and moreover it is not easy save to a player. As for wanton love, it is not worth notation: it is but a fancy which passes as soon as it is consummated. It is wisdom, then, if you are troubled with a wanton and rebellious love, to force the matter to a crisis with such speed as may be, that your mind may the more rapidly uncloud itself to perceive the arts of the world. For who would remain long in the absurd posture of the lover, with his bowings, his musings, his sad airs—this *Malvolio* who is laughed at by all the world, and alone laughs not at himself!

SAME

SAME

MADNESS lies in monotony : men have fallen to suicide from very weariness of doing the same thing. Certainly to go round and round in the same path, at the same task, day after day, like a horse at a mill, without any object but daily bread, and with death as the inevitable end, is not inspiring; so be not surprised if men sometimes go out to meet death. If you have ambitions or a plan, you may do any task however dulling and still respect yourself, since it will not last for always ; but to sweat at some mean work, to bear the scourge of a master, merely for trivial comforts, such as maintaining a suburban cottage, or a seat in church, or a broad-cloth coat, is the most servile of degradations. Better be the pariah-dog who wanders where he listeth, or the gypsy to whom none can say, "I order you." I have often looked at old third or fourth clerks in the counting-houses of the city-merchants, and wondered how, when they were young and their blood was still hot, they had been content to help somebody else

to

to grow rich and powerful, while they saw nothing for themselves beyond the place of third or fourth clerk, and death. Now they are silly and obsequious, or weakly arrogant: their faces are the white flags of their unwholesome surrender. You are under a tyrant if you have to walk in step, to pass through the same street, to arrive at a certain place at a certain hour, year after year against your will. A town, when you cannot get out of it, becomes a prison.

Withal, there is a certain value in iteration. This you will perceive when you consider the advertisements which are now so much in vogue. The advertisement which I see most often, whether it be of a perfume which I never use, or of a lady's "bust-improver" which is no concern of mine, is the one which sticks in my memory. And the low gibing player having raised a laugh with a jest, will repeat the jest again and again as a catchphrase amid the increasing laughter of his audience. Further, (if I may turn thus suddenly from profane things to grave) in the Rosary, a devotion much affected by Catholicks, you are invited to meditate on some mystery, while you mumble continually the *Ave Maria*. Repetition keeps your attention fixed; and since by repetition you have come to know your task perfectly, there is no strain. Nay! many prisoners, rebellious at first, after years of durance do their work without repining, if the
work

work set them be not altogether beyond the compass of their strength.

In great matters custom is good, for it strengthens the sinews. What you have done often without occasion, you will doubtless do well amid excitement. Thus soldiers are drilled in sham battles; and recruits used to powder. Napoleon said, that he had rarely met with "unprepared courage, that "which is necessary on an unexpected occasion, "and in spite of the most unforeseen events, "leaves full freedom of judgment and decision:" and he declared, that as a possessor of this kind of courage he had met with few persons equal to himself. This courage came to him because he lived long in camps, amongst sudden rushings to and fro, and alarums. It is of the valour and resource which spring from custom that Machiavel is thinking when he observes, that if you wish an assassination well achieved, you will choose for instrument not one who boasts of his violence, but rather one whose hands have been already in blood. A condition of success is rehearsal. If you descry far off in your life some deed which belike you will one day have to perform, it were well to fall to practice at once: otherwise, when the time for action arrives, you may be stultified and bemused.

THEN

THEN

I HAVE often wondered at the condescension with which men and women treat children. If the children could obliterate the moustache and the long dresses, they would discover but taller forms of themselves. Man is a child with liberty. The man whose brain has not been debauched by hypocritical thinking must sometimes say when he finds himself sitting up late and talking with authority: Why can I do this now, when I should have been rebuked for this as a child, and should have had to fall back upon long conversations with my fellows in bed—and yet I am the same child! For the years have but covered him as snow covers the earth; and underneath the years he is still ten years old. Save for the mud picked up by contact with the world which is called knowledge and is mainly a knowledge of sin, and with some (with some only, since you encounter foolish old men) the learning which is a matter of added years, men are as children. Scrape this crust from yourself, and you will find (to your surprise perhaps) a child. To your surprise; for you thought

thought the decades had done more for you: that you were in the act of founding a character, when you were only building laboriously on foundations laid long ago. You are in the position of one who returns to a city after an absence of ten years, and is indignant that the streets shew no mark of change. Wherefore, then, the air of superiority towards children, since you are but a child *plus* a few vices? Children are sent to bed for making a noise at their game: men shout over their wine, and women cackle with laughter in the drawing-room. Where is the difference? But you puff your cheeks and say: I am a man! You pose for Jupiter; you are only Jupiter *Scapin*. When you were a child you said: This I will do when I am a man: and still you say, This I will do; but the last part of the sentence dwindles to a sigh.

Since you are still a child, it is foolish to repine for things that are gone. The past has no more to do with you than the hair the barber cut from your head yesterday. Life is largely a matter not of renunciations, as some hold, but of repudiations. Time compels you to discharge cargo. At twenty you loved to dream for hours on the desolate shore, watching the tall masts of the ships; at twenty-five you will not be alone a minute if you can help it—you are all for action and the haunts of men. At twenty you loved Olive with the dusky hair; at
twenty-five

twenty-five it is Blanche with the lily hands. If you are an artist, that work is alone tolerable which you are now doing; and you hate to think of what you did last year. Every year scrawls Disgust in large letters across the face of the one that preceded it. An old man will tell you that if he had his life to live over again he would live it differently. Radically you are the same at this time of life as at that; but you wear other clothes and you think you are another man. In truth, past things are the mere dust we have raised by our rushing wheels, and in general, are no more to be regarded than the dust. When the whole past becomes the present, at the hour of death, it can be no more than a film. Whether a life has been imbued with religion, duty, and prosperous love, or immasked with contempt of these elements, must be unimportant when the years pass like seconds before dying eyes. Even power and success, those rivets of an active life, become vulgar beside the death-bed.

Still, there are some things which you have done in the past, when you had lost the wisdom of childhood and ere you had come to a knowledge of the arts of men, which if you are sensitive must haunt the memory with despairing gestures. You have crouched at an insult, or you have battled unwisely. You have let an advantage slip, or you have neglected to intrench yourself. But these things are too little to be noted; and are fitter to
be

be whispered in the confessional than for serious observation. Yet trifles sting; and in lonely moments you blush and squirm beneath them. Even a heedless *gaucherie* committed under hostile eyes (and most eyes are hostile) can make you feel, if you look back at it, a poignant anguish.

WHITE

WHITE

THE snow which had fallen in the night lay dry upon the ground, and the sun was shining as I entered the house. In the hall and on the stairs were flowers—summer flowers on the bright winter day: lilies of the valley, and faint gardenias, and garlands of white roses. A grave man handed me a pair of gloves. From a room came a murmur of voices—the voices of those who were here for the funeral. In the hall and on the stairs was the smell of flowers, mingled with the smell of new cloth stuffs. I went up the stairs, and opened the door of a room. It was hung with lace. In one corner of the room was a bed covered with a sheet. In the middle of the room was something which stood on trestles; and the six pure wax candles which surrounded it were almost burned out, for they had been burning all night. It was hard to distinguish their little flames amid the glare of the sunlight and the snow which streamed through the windows. Here again were flowers: lilies of the valley, and faint gardenias, and garlands of white roses. A tall woman, with gray hair and a wan tortured

tortured face, rose up from the foot of the bier where she had been kneeling. It was the mother. As she passed out, Hugo's lines ran into my head:

> "L'enfant n'est plus là, madame, qu'en faire?
> Faites-en un drap pour m'ensevelir."

I was alone with the dead. I went over and looked at her—the beautiful girl whose laugh was like the dreamy echo of cascades—where she lay rigid, in her awful passionless purity, with her glorious hair like a mantle over her shoulders. What dream was passing behind her face that she looked so serious—so serious and even unhappy! Could this thing be her home for evermore—would she not spring up in a moment and open frightened eyes, and then, like a child released from a dark room, half laughing and crying tell us of her tremours? Peace. But ah! her purity—her holy, marvellous purity! I wandered to the window. A troop of children with white veils on their heads were passing to the church through the snow on their way to their first communion. And still she was dead. I took a lily by its long stem and placed it between her hands, and I smiled. Of a sudden, some black-robed figures clouded the whiteness of the room, and filled it with their weeping. They wept—they wept; and through their weeping I smiled.

BE

BE

IT is written whether your life is to be a tragedy or a vaudeville. All is settled; you can but adjust the details. You are no more the moving power of your being, than you are of the assassin's arm which (it may be) is to strike you down. The arrangement of the details is what is left to you, and only of the details which concern your own self. In other men's businesses you are a foreigner and suspected. Hence it is unwise to get in front of the headlong man. If your brother or your sister is rushing to foolishness, stand aside, lest you be caught in the wheels. Moreover, they will ruthlessly drive over you, and continue their downhill passage with your futile blood on their axle. Strive to stay the movements of the stars, and you shall be ground to powder. The stars have forced certain ones to descend: who are you that you should interrupt the journey?

In life you must practice what arts you wot of; for though the end is determined, yet it is more happily reached by good means. In this you are like a boy who shall certainly come to know his lesson

lesson after some hours by diligent conning of the dictionary and grammar, and yet would take the easier road of a prohibited translation, and so the sooner to play. To play in life is to rule; and you arrive at ruling by art. Cæsar and Richelieu came to great place by being more artful than their fellows. A prime art is to find out what you can do best, and to stick at it despite inclination and criticism. What we do best is not often what we like to do best. I myself write verse and prose (whether I do it well or not is without the question)—but I write verse and prose because it is the work to which my hand lends itself most deftly. It is not my inclination: I have to do something, and I would rather not do this: I had rather be a foreman in a yard who shouts at other men, or a captain of a merchant-ship, or a general with an army of fifty thousand men under him, than a writer of verse and prose. But with words I am most at ease; so it is my part to set them in order, while it is your's, perhaps, to do one of the other things I have mentioned.

In relation to this matter, it is to be noted, that there is a certain subtle pride which sometimes leads men of birth to declare that they would with pleasure be menials. And you may find a gentleman, when he is driven to it, blacking boots and emptying slops without compunction; while the soul of a churl revolts at these tasks. Of course the reason

reason is, that the man of pedigree deems himself already so high that he cannot possibly be brought below the level of those for whom he opens doors; while the base-born man who has (as they say) "raised himself," recoils from the uniform of the footman, since he has a temper to appreciate the servility it describes. Of the aristocratic mood was Thackeray when he said, that he would like to have been Shakespeare's shoe-black: and the increase in our time of the opposite mood is shewn by the decay of the mode (at present used only by very proud and high folk) of subscribing oneself in one's letters as the servant of the person to whom one is writing. The Pope, being in high place, signs himself, "The servant of the servants of "God:" and this put me in mind to say how much of what is called spiritual humility is really a wily pride. You will read in some of the lives of the saints, how this saint wore an old and ragged habit which had been discarded by other monks, and how that saint washed the dishes for his monastery; and you are invited to ponder on the humility of the saints. But you are to consider that since these saints were working for God, and knew that their brethren knew it, the sting was withdrawn from their abject deeds. For the sting of servility is contempt; and no man is fool enough to be contemptuous of one who is playing wisely for a great stake. When a saint, to win Heaven, allowed himself

self to be scourged in the chapter-room, or peeled potatoes in the kitchen, he stood no more chance of being despised than a powerful minister does who flatters his king that he may gain a celebrated cause. The saint is in the position of a soldier who (far from thinking himself demeaned) is proud to take orders from a victorious general; and this position is very different from that of the drudge who fawns on a brutal house-master. Nay! a Pope can wash the feet of twelve poor pilgrims without one really humble thought: the descent is so steep that he adequately values his height: and when he once more assumes the tiara and presents his toe, the effect is that of a recreation.

VAH!

VAH!

(For Aubrey Beardsley's Picture, "The Litany of Mary Magdalen")

SHE has set up her lectern in the street. In the public ways, in the stinging glare of the sun, she does penance; and the dust is hot in her mouth. Far off are trees, but their pleasant shade is not for her; nor for her the river with its murmuring coolness. The humming magic of the world sounds not in her ears; and the pomps of life are become as the burthen of some half-forgotten song. Imploring, despairing, in stern grief, she chaunts her passionate litany. Her eyes are faded and tired; her hair is tarnished; but her soul—ah! her soul is floating on a delicate sea, amongst the courageous sons of God. Those whom she knew yesterday, men and women with whom she has sinned, pass by, and recognizing her devotion, lash her with scornful gibes. What bitter jeers they cast in her teeth!—jeers more bitter than ashes; more bitter than love grown a-weary, and the lees of wine; bitterer far than fasting and tears. But she

she looks neither to the right nor the left: she will not—she dare not hearken to the mocking voices: louder and louder she chaunts—she shrieks her supplication in heart-quaking tones: anything to drown the voices, anything that she may not take pause and think. She is wan with a subtile terror of the morbific touch which can change the devout phrases of her rogation into something perverse and awry—a penitential prayer for having repented. She knows that if she loiters to consider, she will be lost. Has she not looked deeply into *His* eyes and seen the terror of the generations of man as they go to death? Has she not felt the tumult, when to a blare of trumpets a mighty throne uprears itself amidst the throng, upon which is seated, potent and thunderous, the unveiled form of God the Father? Has she not seen this in *His* eyes; and felt for *Him* a wonderful consuming love, beside which all other loves have dwindled and shuddered to mere lust? Louder and louder she chaunts, while the rays of the sun stab her like spears of steel; clinging to the lectern she testifies, while the gibes scourge her like little knotted cords. Dimly she sees before her the shadow of a face—a wan, agonized face crowned with thorns; and looking on that face she makes of her passion a joyful martyrdom.

And thou, O beautiful girl, whose eyes are laden with sorrow and yearning, who standest aside making

making no part with the scoffers—ah! what is to be thy fate? Shall the Holy Ghost alight upon thy heart and fill thee with the melody of divine song? Or shalt thou, rather, having looked on the penitent say: "I would, but I am not strong enough;" and turning sadly go down the steep street, till thou comest to the Potter's Field which is at the end of it, and lie there without hope of the resurrection of the dead?

WEAR

WEAR

YOU will see at a pantomime a player who assumes so many masks, that at no time, or perhaps only once, does he present his real visage to the beholders. His ruse is to befog the spectators by his protean glidings, till they come to believe that they have seen through him the nature and characteristics of various men. In like wise your life must be masked and covered by appearances. It is fatal to appear at all times as you are, since faces relate more than words. But before we speak of that, certain it is that if you wish the world to take heed of your ideas, you must, in uttering them, be garbed in a coat cut to the fashion. The world is silly enough to suppose that genius is never shabby, or is never otherwise than shabby, as the case may be. If you plan financial or political reform, you must, to make your cause good with the world, be as neatly polished as any cavalry officer; if you are a poet or a painter, you must carry a dreamy eye, a dirty shirt, and vagrant hair. The rich man smells a suitor in the unkempt reformer; and the most urbane

urbane hostess will turn a wry and disappointed face to an artist, if she find him with customs and a costume remote from the dance-halls of Montmartre. No matter for the public good can lie in the threadbare, no poetry or musick in the decent! says the world: and only those who have won, or the very strong, dare to thrust their tongues in their cheeks and deny the world as a soothsayer. But it is to be noted, that the world has not seldom been caught in its own toils: for a glossy raiment often covers the thievish adventurer; and the accepted presentment of the poet has led the credulous to value highly the small wares of some ignorant and simpering impostor.

These are but marks of the trivial side of appearances which appeal to the foolish part of men's minds, but, nevertheless, are to be studied, since mankind is largely foolish. Clothes are the comedy of masking: but the different faces you are to school yourself to shew abroad at different times deserve persistent study. Unless you have sedulously practised, your face can be nothing but a confessing flag which advises an enemy where to fire. The rules which the Jesuits are said to observe, such as placing one with whom you are conversing in a strong light, while you yourself sit in the shade with downcast eyes, are all good points of wisdom: but it is only a sorry by-word of the streets which attributes these arts to the Jesuits, who

who are (as any one who has been much in their company can testify) mostly simple men. Disraeli, being once attacked to weariness for permitting the Jesuits to go about at will in England, "I have "heard" (says he) "that it is a practice of the Jesuits "to set lay-brothers at large to disparage their "Order." With these words he silenced his tormentors; and shewed by making a statement which he did not himself believe, but many dupes would believe as he wished them to believe, that he was a master (like most great men) of the wiles which dullards are wont to call Jesuitical, seeking thereby to put an affront on the Jesuits. If I were a concealed Jesuit, and if the Jesuits were what some folk still think they are, it would be an excellent piece of wiliness to write as I am writing now, so that you might be unguarded, and come to accept the Society as contemplative and without guile. But, as I say, the Jesuits have no arts.

Now as to the face, it is well to shape yourself to an impassive mien, so that you present the same front at a bridal and at a funeral. This is much in favour with gamesters, and those who play at cards. Still, sudden starts at hearing a thing you know well, and quietude and indifference at hearing of some disaster for the first time, are good if you are not alone when you get the news, since they are ruses which baffle the onlookers. If you have reason to think that a man intends by a speech to deal you a shocking blow, look your hardest at Medusa, and send him away empty. I knew a wise man who used to give forth volumes of anger whenever he heard a tale of cruelty; so that people, falling into his snare, went about proclaiming his kind heart. Yet he was in reality a tyrant whose hand itched for a sceptre of iron. I once had an opportunity to observe a nun; and I noticed, with much admiration, that whenever she began to feel any emotion, whether of pleasure or anger, she at once lowered the lids over her eyes. If the eyes are the windows of the soul, we have always blinds which we can pull down when the soul is undressed.

CRAVE

CRAVE

I

EVERY morning three tire-women of great beauty came to the apartments of the King's mistress. They would spread before her a number of pleasant gowns, so that she might choose the ones she would wear at different hours in the day. When she had chosen her dresses, or, if she chanced to be too lazy for decision, had made her women decide for her, she rose and went into her cool, fragrant bath-room. After she had bathed, her women rubbed her white body with lavender-scented water; and when she was half-dressed she passed to another room to have her hair brushed. The day had grown middle-aged when she came to sit in one of the windows of the palace and look out languidly with her chin in her hands at a long grassy avenue bordered with trees. Believe me, I endeavour to write staidly, with the sandy dryness of a legal code, to narrate and not to expatiate, or I would tell you how lovely she was as she sat there with her marvellous hair sweeping above her oval face, her thin hands, and her puzzling eyes
which

which had the shyness and colour of violets. Her women were indeed beautiful; but their beauty seemed niggard, a little common, when they were in the company of the King's mistress.

She sat waiting for the King to come, and looking up the green avenue that seemed to have no end but the blue sky. Of what was she thinking as she sat there so quietly with her chin between her hands? Were her thoughts with the King—with him whom an elegant writer would call "her royal "lover"? Perhaps. Or perhaps she was dreaming of her small shabby home, of her mother's sewing, of all the wretched time when her life seemed to be impaled on a needle, before she became an opera dancer. For it was at the opera that the King had first seen her; and she had given herself to him not in any heat of love, but prudently and after due season of waiting. The King was exceeding prone to violent amours; but so inflamed was he by his latest mistress that for two years she had swayed the Court without a rival. But (it is really too nice a question to ask) had she any love for the King?

II

In the King's Body-guard, the flower of his army, there was a young man of unusual beauty. Call to mind the adorable pensiveness of the Antinous at the Vatican, and the divine alertness and fire of the Apollo, and you will have glanced at this exquisite youth. He had large eyes which turned from blue to black with his mood; a complexion like roses asleep in cream; and curling golden hair. He was lithe, and active, and supple as a deerhound. His features were extremely delicate; and as he had none of that air of assurance which is supposed to be a part of the handsome man, he looked a little like a girl in a uniform, and he had all the niceties and sedulous care of his appearance that a girl might have shewn in his place. He was merely a soldier in the ranks, the son of a peasant, and it pains me to have to add that he did not speak the King's language with a good accent, or even correctly. One day the High Chamberlain of the Palace came before the King with a mighty grave face, and stated that he had intercepted glances full of love between the King's mistress and this young soldier.

"You lie," said the King simply. He was a despot, and as he had no parliament to annoy him, he took his ease with his officials.

The

The High Chamberlain proposed to lay his head on the scaffold if what he said was not true. Let the King put the matter to the proof. He would arrange that the soldier was put on guard in the passage through which the mistress passed to the royal apartments from her own; and then, if his majesty would condescend to watch, he would see a thing. Sure enough, as the mistress tripped along the passage, thinking herself unperceived she threw a languishing glance at the youth, and sent him a kiss from her finger-tips; while he, in his turn, looked so sentimental that he might have represented in allegory Love conquering Timidity.

"Are you unhappy?" the King asked his mistress. "Is there anything you wish for very, very much?"

She hung her head and said she was quite happy. Then she began to weep. The King took her in his arms and encouraged her. After a time she confessed that she loved a soldier in the King's Body-guard, and that, though the King should kill her, she could never love any one else.

"I have loved him for two months," she sobbed.

"So long?" said the King. "It must be a real passion. Let the soldier be brought before us."

The mistress flung herself at the King's feet and implored him to have pity on her lover. When the soldier stood trembling in the royal closet, the King

King took the hand of his mistress and placed it in that of the young man.

"Of course you will marry," said the King. "You may live in any part of my realm that you like, and no man shall harm you. But I am afraid you will be very poor," he added considerately.

The lovers were full of gratitude, and protested that they welcomed poverty, since they were rich in love. When they had retired: "Your majesty has shewn great clemency," quoth the High Chamberlain.

The King pursed his mouth and looked on the ground. "I wonder?" he said at last, and smiled with his upper lip.

III

TEN years after, the King, who had been hunting, found himself astray in the forest as the day grew to an end, with no attendant near him save the Grand Huntsman. I ought to mention that the King had changed very much in these ten years: his beard, for one thing, had grown, and his hair was touched with gray. Now when he and the Grand Huntsman perceived that they were far from the rest of the party, and that their horses were spent and in need of water, they endeavoured with some anxiety to find a woodlander's hut where they might rest and learn the right path. For some time they rode in silence through the dim murmuring forest in the twilight, till at last they came suddenly upon a clearing in which stood a house. But what a house! The windows were broken and stuffed with rags; the chimney was crumbling, and the roof clamoured for repair; the door swung loosely on a rusty hinge. Three or four squalid children were playing in front of the house, and there were evidently some more within. The whole place spoke not of a neat labouring poverty, but rather of a growing degradation which the owners were too apathetic to avert. The King rapped on the door with the handle of his whip. A loose-lipped, mottled-faced woman appeared with her hair

hair in disorder. She was carrying a child in her arms, and was big with another. She did not know the King; but she made no difficulty about doing what she was asked when the Grand Huntsman shewed that he was willing to pay her. They followed her to an inner room where a man sat, without a coat, doing nothing. He had a fat face, sensual and gross; fat creases were under his eyes; and his fat, dirty hands rested on his knees. He and the woman resumed a quarrel which had been interrupted by the arrival of the strangers. Without considering the presence of the new-comers, they hurled at each other the most atrocious insults. She raged at the man's miserable, petty infidelities; and he replied by shamelessly gibing at her prolific motherhood. The Grand Huntsman thought the whole scene sufficiently odious.

"You see what I have come to, gentlemen," said the woman, turning suddenly to the King and his companion. "You wouldn't believe to look at me that I was once a king's mistress, and that my word was law in the palace. Oh, yes, I was all that!—the King worshipped me. And I gave it up to marry that low brute over there because I loved him. I was caught by his pretty face—he has a pretty face now, hasn't he? My God, my God, what a life I have had!"

"Hold your tongue!" yelled the man. "If you hadn't thrown yourself at my head I might now be captain of the King's Body-guard."

They

They continued the row, shouting and banging the table, and pouring out the most abominable injuries. At last the woman said something so intimate, so wounding, that the man rose, blind with fury, and seizing the lamp he flung it at her with all his strength. Amid the screams that followed the crash of broken glass, the King and the Grand Huntsman left the cottage.

"She said she was a king's mistress," said the Grand Huntsman doubtfully, as they rode through the dark forest.

"She *was*," replied the other significantly; "but I am still the King."

This was enigmatical, and the Grand Huntsman was baffled: but who was he to question the King? They went on for a while without speaking; and the shadows grew thicker.

"If what that woman said was true," the Grand Huntsman ventured to observe after they had ridden about a mile, "and if she was idiot enough to reject a king's love because she was in love with some man, she deserves the worst fate. She has struck the gods in the face. What a mad-woman! what a suicide!"

The King looked pleased. "You see the truth of things with refreshing clearness, Grand Huntsman," he said. "You shall certainly be decorated on our next birthday."

WRITHE

WRITHE

THE Mute has a seat, sometimes a throne, in the breast of most adults. You shall encounter many who rejoice in blacks, and obsequies, and funeral meats; and this not from a horror of death, which sometimes produces (strangely enough) necrophilial spasms (as one who sees something dire inevitably approaching, trains his mind to welcome it, and even to like it, so that its passing may be less terrible)—no; not from a horror of death, and not from reverence, but because the emotion of tears is to them delicious. Some have a low passion for assuming the griefs of others. Your sorrow is their joy; and they will kill you your friend many times over in the course of a night. Nay! even if you be too wise to mourn, they will impertinently consider that you must be mourning. To these the death of a king or of a statesman is an immense boon. "The poor king—how I pity the dear queen!" they cry with heavy sobs, and think about their dinner. And if they find themselves in such ill case as to have no grief, public or private, to weep over, they hie them

to

to a theatre and watch the feignings and contortions of some player. Wherefore St. Augustine speaking of stage-plays, "Why is it" (he asks) "that man "desires to be there made sad, beholding grievous "and tragical things, which yet himself would by no "means suffer? Yet he desires as a spectator to feel "grief at them, and this very grief is his pleasure." I object to the obviously lachrymose, and I oppose to their clamours the saying of Napoleon who, when Talleyrand said to him, on the news of the death of the boy who was thought to be the heir of his empire, that he doubtless felt very sad: "I do not "amuse myself," replied Bonaparte, "by thinking of "dead people."

But of matters that bring real gloom, there are two kinds: the things that happen, and the things that you suspect. And there are two degrees of this suspicion. The first is positive, when a man fears that he is threatened with disaster and walks abroad under menaces. The second is negative, when a man looks back over his life and shudders at the mistakes he has made. For the first of these, it is indeed idle, and the most sickly dreaming to go in dread of what is not arrived and of what may never arrive. You are to consider, that if it is written that a thing is to fall upon you, the blow cannot be avoided for all your writhing. If on the other hand, your destiny is to escape the blow, no threats can give it impetus. If you are moody and alarmed,
you

you will do well to cultivate the principle of attack. Open yourself to those whom you fear, playing against them what advantages you possess, even if by doing so you bring the matter to an issue. For there is no ill in the world so monstrous as our apprehensions of ill. The instinct of the wretch condemned to death tells him this; and he sighs, not because the days between him and his doom pass too quickly, but because they do not pass quickly enough. Sit lonely with your dreadful thoughts, and they will ride you haggard.

As for the second or negative part of this suspicion, I would have you realize that you lament the errors of your life chiefly because they have been perceived by others. But it were good to reflect that men are so occupied with the garbage in their own bosoms, that they give only a careless attention to your affairs. You stare at some pigmy mistake till before your disordered sight it rises a giant: in anguish you think the world is gazing with astonishment at the giant—but you are deceived: for the world it is still a pigmy.

But in some things that do happen you have matter enough for wringing your hands. How can a contained pen describe such miseries? You have hung about the ante-rooms of the powerful; you have sued humbly and servilely some petty favour from a man you despise; you have stood his insolence, his sneers, you have laughed abjectly at his jokes

jokes—this you have done and you have not struck him dead: you have cowered like a cur. You have seen him throw mud upon what you hold dear; you have heard him flaunt your ideals; and then you have had his refusal, and the gibes of his underlings—ah God! ah God! it brings out a sweat of blood. Happier, oh, far happier, the lot of a prisoner of Carthage bent back upon a steel stake, and rotting naked beneath a broiling sun. You have done the deed, and not all the perfumes of Arabia can cleanse you; you have done the deed, and the hot shame of it clings to your life like the disgrace of a blow taken and not returned; like a fetid disease; like a loathsome ulcerous sore. Rather than again pass beneath that yoke, you shall kill yourself, with your own applause thundering in your ears.

GOOD

GOOD

ON a certain railway journey which I made some time since, the carriage in which I travelled was shared with an old work-woman. As we were alone, and as she hardly looked at me, I had a chance to observe her narrowly. She was clad in the meanest garments; a soiled cap just managed to cover her gray hairs; on her feet, evident beneath her short skirt, were clogs. Her face, wrinkled and seamed, was a dusky red from exposure to the sun and bitter weather; most of her teeth were gone, and what remained were black fangs; and she had no eyebrows. Her coarse toil-worn hands, frost-bitten and disfigured, lay inert on her lap, like things she was carrying in spite of herself. In her eyes was a dull hopeless stare. She looked like one who had broken stones and eaten dust all the way down the road of life, and found misery at the end of it.

The train stopped at a wayside station, and some people entered the carriage. There were three men and two women. I think the men were painters who had been painting in the forest. One of the

the women, crude and insignificant, seated herself in front of me. The other, exquisitely beautiful, charmingly dressed, gathered up her skirts gingerly and placed herself opposite the old woman. She had that virginal face which is so often seen in those who are not virgins. Her rich hair was arranged in heavy bands falling over the ears: a mode which an opera-dancer had then made the fashion. After a while she drew off one of her gloves and shewed a white, wonderfully shaped hand adorned with gemmed rings. Whether the gems in the rings were real or false I cannot tell; and it matters little.

Distracted by the entrance of the new-comers, I had ceased to gaze at the old woman; but when I looked at her again, I confess that her face somewhat alarmed me. Her eyes had regained their lustre and she was glaring hungrily, even angrily, at the girl's hand. She looked at the girl's dainty hand, and then she looked at her own machines of toil. She looked at the girl's costume, and plucked at her own mean gown. The girl let a well made boot peep from under her skirt, and with that the old woman stood her clogs on heel.

The men who were with the girl seemed good fellows enough; but they were under that excitement which pervades the average man when he is a-holidaying with his intimates. It was due to this, no doubt, that one of them threw some light dis-
paraging

paraging word at the old woman, and looked at the girl for comment. The girl smiled lazily, and just lifted her eyebrows in a contemptuous glance at the old thing in the corner. And upon that, the old woman gave a yell of pain with a kind of sob in it (the sound of which, I must admit, disturbed me for many a day) and seizing the hand of the girl with both her own, began to bite it with her horrible gums.

Of course they pulled her off before she could do much damage, and as we ran into a station at that moment, she was hustled out of the train. The place we had come to being my destination, I also alighted; and when I observed the old woman toiling painfully up the steep hill which led from the railway, I started to overtake her. She was wringing her hands as I drew near, and muttering passionately, and the tears were shining on her weary old face. She recognized in me her fellow-passenger, and burst out into voluble extenuations.

"I didn't mean to hurt her; the good God knows I didn't mean to hurt her! But you saw the rings on her fingers, and what a fine lady she was, and she despised me because I'm an old work-woman. Oh yes, I've worked—I've worked for sixty-five years— Jesus! how I've worked from four in the morning till ten at night. And I've got nothing—nothing, you understand; and she's got all that, and a soft bed,

bed, and nothing to do, just by——." (Here she used a phrase which I will not startle your politeness by repeating). "Why, *I* might have done that, and had white bread every day and good wine to drink—I used to be just as fine as she is. She needn't despise me! When I was at the inn, I tell you, the count offered to take me away with him. Yes! But I thought I'd be sage and marry Jules. What a fool! What a fool! Tell me, did you see her hair?—look at mine!" She flung off her cap and trampled it in the dust, and her gray wisps of hair hung lank on her head. "Did you see her little white hand with the clean pink nails and the rings? Very well then—look at my hands!" She held them out trembling, the fingers knotted with rheumatism, the nails broken and black. I turned away. You know the adage.

HELP

HELP

IN general, to help a man is like reviving an assassin who has designs on your life. For beyond the truth that most men are naturally your enemies, the one who solicits your help shews by the very act that you have something which he has not, and which he cannot like you for having. And what do you gain? Not gratitude surely; for gratitude is only a theory. No man, outside of play-books and romances, feels grateful to another who has done him a favour. Nay! if he think about your favour at all, he thinks you might have done more. A sense of obligation engenders a sense of hate. Further, the man who asks you for money or assistance has, in many cases, been to others, more astute, who have refused him before he comes to you; so while he takes your help he considers you his dupe. Nor does he hesitate to belittle you abroad; for he has an uneasy feeling that you have beheld him abject, and he wishes other men to see you on a level. Languages bristle with proverbs concerning the foolishness of lenders and the levity of borrowers.

Certainly, it is the grossest and clumsiest of
follies

follies to help a man who is striving towards the same goal as yourself. For by seeking your aid he makes it clear that you have already got the better of him; and by coming to his succour you bring him the means not only to right himself, but to draw up abreast of you, and even to leave you a distance in the rear. Worse still, when he has once got ahead of you, he will doubtless fling stumbling-blocks in your path. And though he come to greatness, yet will you not have his thanks: for men when they reach a pinnacle think not of the ladder, or only to throw it down, so that no other may ascend. Rather will he abhor you, and seek your degradation, as one who has made him fetch his breath. Hence Machiavel draws the axiom that "he who is the cause of another's greatness is himself undone." A merchant who aids one in his own trade who has fallen on difficulties, deserves himself to fail; for he places a weapon in the hands of a rival whom fate had conveniently disarmed. As monstrous a folly, but one more clearly perceived by mankind, is to assist or be kind to those whom you fear; for by this you expose your tremours, and shew the threateners that you go in awe of their menaces, and value them so far that you are compelled to do what you would not.

Now as for those whom it is wise to help: they are men who are of use to you, and who are held by by your aid, since they know that if you be lost to them, they will get nothing from others. Wherefore their interest jumps with your service. And it is a good caution not to give them too much, but just enough to keep them sedulous while they must remain inferior; for, as Bacon has it, "there "is little friendship in the world, and least of all "between equals." And I would urge upon you, that the moment a man says (whether in anger or pleasantry) that he can do as well without your assistance, cut him off. Your bounty is profitably spent only on the dependent. Again, it is politic to help those who you are sure will spread the rumour of your generosity, so that you may have the fame of your good deeds. I knew one who, whenever he had helped a man, would say to him (looking meanwhile demure) "I hope you have "not mentioned it;" and when the other replied that he had, "Why, then you did wrong," says the first, with some marks of anger, yet shewing he was not displeased. And to conclude this, it is wise to help (if you be asked) those who are sure to succeed, yet not in your own way of life, so that their success will not be your injury. Otherwise you may find yourself in the position of Chesterfield, who having set Johnson at naught and turned him out of doors, afterwards sued to have Johnson's great Dictionary dedicated to him, and had to stomach an insolent refusal.

RUSH

RUSH

HASTE is the negation of dignity. This you will perceive if you go to a railway station and watch late people hurrying to catch a train; which, if they lose, they stand fuddled, mopping their brows, confessed fools in the sight of men. To lose a train after you have strained every nerve to gain it, is one of the great mistakes of life in little. If, on the other hand, you saunter to the place of departure, and, refusing to run, gaze on the train as it glides away with calm eyes, you do not apprize a jeering crowd that you have been defeated. To be leisurely is an act of faith and also an act of liberty: for if you do not hasten towards an end you shew that you believe in your star, and messengers under orders run. Moreover, haste implies eagerness; and it is not well to acquaint the world that you are eager after anything, for then it looks to see you fall.

This is against hasty and futile appearance, which is by no means to be confounded with promptitude of action. The prompt to act and seize are not often the hurried. It is a good point of wisdom to
arrange

arrange your plans in tranquillity so that when the time comes for quick action you may appear to your opponents indolent and trifling. This manner you can compass by making sure that your schemes, arranged beforehand, are working; and it is certain to disconcert others. Thus Disraeli was wont to assume, in the heat of debate, a languid accent and frivolity of phrase, to hide the fact that he desired some advantage, or that he meditated vigorous action. And I knew a woman who never failed in any enterprise, however arduous, she undertook, although she was free at all times from the least trace of hurry. This because she had her plans compact in her head, and could afford to study, as it were idly, the dishevelled projects of her rivals. The dandies, like Brummel and d'Orsay (from whom, indeed, Disraeli copied much), whose theory it was that we should never let our emotions run out of harness, shewed again and again how a light word flung lazily into the air could bring discomfiture to the heated man. So shall you see a vain fellow, who has thought to overwhelm you by his angry speech, put out of order if you drop a cold and measured word, and go backward and forward in vague and inane prolixity.

Haste is good and profitable when it is not felt, but put on as a mask. Thus, if a troublesome suitor is plaguing you with his importunities, 'tis well to plead that you are engaged with one who
will

will brook no dallying, and presently rush off as though you were pursued. Or if there is a letter or other document which you are interested to destroy, it is a good ruse to feign great anger, and in midst of a rush of words, to seize the paper suddenly and hurl it into the fire as though blinded by hasty rage to the import of what you are doing. Finally, it is happier to be speedy rather than lingering in the matter of death; for the mile before death is thronged with ghosts, and one who travels fast hears not their mournful, pitiless voices.

SEED

SEED

THE sun of a wintry afternoon was just turning crimson, and touching with reluctant ardourless rays the trees and the hay-stacks, as she rounded a corner of the road and came to a stand in the village street. She stood in front of the little shop where tobacco and small necessities were sold: a pitiable figure, shameful, unshapely, a target for scorn. Her great blue eyes were only timidly defiant for the casual; but they were also beseeching for the close observer, to whom they seemed to say: I repel you; but—but if you were not repelled, I could weep on your shoulder. She smoothed in some fashion her yellow hair with her coarse, frost-bitten hand, and pulled her wretched shawl down over her waist, attempting to hide (the attempt was futile, and she knew it) her condition from the accusing eyes of those who knew her. Then she looked up and down wearily. The village had altered not at all, she thought with vague disappointment; after her months of exile, so long and important for her, how placid it remained, how little changed! Although, in truth, in her wanderings

ings she had been but slightly extravagant—the most outlying farm at which she had worked was not more than a dozen miles away—still, to her rustic, home-keeping mind it seemed that she had been upon a perilous journey, and she felt cheated that on a return which clamoured for change, she found none. And the villagers, were they too unchanged? She had thought of them so much in the last months, had dreamed often and often of meeting them as of old, of an intercourse which should never recall her offence. No; they could not be changed: at the worst they would ignore her—let her go by, give her leave to work, and perhaps (who knows?) to die in peace when her time came. It was this thought which had led her home again.

The people in the shop, at any rate, had seen her without any sign of welcome or hostility: she was a mark for their scrutiny—they must be talking of her not otherwise than reproachfully, she felt; and her face burned. Three girls with whom she had been intimate, red-cheeked, fleshly creatures, noisy with the mirth of the country-side, came towards her down the road; who, when they sighted her, went by staidly, hushing their laughter. After them, in a little while, came a tall, gray-haired woman with deep compassionate eyes, carrying a milk-pail. "Well, my girl, back again?" she murmured, distantly yet sadly, and brushed by quickly, alarmed

alarmed at her good-nature. The woman before the shop moved a few paces sluggishly, and looked back on the hurrying figure. Ah, that one too! She had known yon old woman all her life; had fed at her table, worked by her side, slept with her in her bed. Now, for the first time, she realized the anguish which public censure brings to all but the most resolute; the doubts, the furious anger, the grinding sense of injustice, the strange humility, which mingle in the leper's ostracism. She carried lightly any religious conviction of sin: her thought of God included—nay! was contained in her thought of a lukewarm parson disgusted with his meagre country living: but she was very clear about the moral code of her village, and she was compelled to face the fact (a heaving breast and tears came with the naked horror of it) that she had sinned deeply against her tribe—against her *commune*. She wished passionately that she had not come back, that she had remained to die amongst those who, to her, were a stranger people. Starting from a different ground, her agony and repentance were as acute and sincere as that of any follower of the Mystical Theology; and it may be hazarded that had she been presented to St. Teresa, the author of "The Way of Perfection" would not have denied the value—more valuable, almost, because so Godless and ignorant—of her abnegation. A man wearing "leggings" came out of of the "Nag's Head" opposite, and stood in the middle of the road jeering at her; then, when he grew tired, he turned back to the inn. The doctor, a young man with a black beard, drove by in his gig, and she regarded him with a new sensation, an interest which was near to pain. Would not he, that young man, have intimate, necessary relations with her at the supreme moment which every hour brought closer?—a moment as important for her as the morning of battle is for the famous commander. The man who had flouted her came out from the inn with five or six more laughing and talking violently; then they parted, straggling off in different ways, calling to one another from a distance. The day faded and died in the sky with a last wild light which told of coming storm.

As the dusk thickened, she thought she would go over to the inn and ask the landlady, to whom she was known, to give her out of pity a lodging. People might be hard, even cruel to her; but must they not have a tenderness for the mystery she carried within her, that thing which was alive though yet unborn? A mother's thought! She failed to perceive that when folk gibed at her shame, they gibed more particularly at the fruit of her shame; she failed to note, above all, that people are never quite surely interested in what is not their own, and that she had never consulted anybody as to her right to bring another creature into

into this suffering world. Women to whom this tremendous power is given (a power greater than that of the greatest kings who have ruled the earth) are slow to realize their responsibility, if indeed they ever think of it. As a rule, they shirk the thought that they deliberately give birth to a creature who may become insane or an habitual drunkard, who may lie in gaol for years a convicted felon, who may stand under a scaffold, and who shall certainly have his full share of the general pain and misery. It is difficult to see how the mother of a murderer after he is hanged, can escape feeling, in some sort, like a murderer herself. But, like most mothers, the rustic who is being dealt with thought of none of these things—only felt incoherently, but very strongly, how glad she would be to have a child; how she would work for it, and love it, and treasure it, and treasure herself too, now, for its sake. So she crossed the road painfully, haltingly (she had hurt her foot upon her tramp homeward), and had found the latch of the inn door, when she heard her name tossed about by many voices, and attached to it an epithet which, to her simple thinking, was reserved for the most vile. They were coming, these people, from all points: the whole village, it seemed to her as she peered through the dim uncertain light, had turned out to reprove her—to resent her presence there. The men she had seen leaving the inn had gone, it was evident,

evident, to tell of her re-entrance and to rouse their homes; for there they were in the front of the procession, exulting in their leadership, ripe for dastardly mischief. They were coming for her, to examine her, doubtless to jeer at her, to ask her to go: and when she made sure of all that a great fear came over her, not for herself—she was sick and hopeless enough—but for the thing which was become part of her, the life which depended on her life. Surely they would not hurt her child!—in her terror she felt as if she were already carrying it in her arms. In the churchyard lay the calm witnessing dead—her own dead amongst them—rebuking by their quietism, their detachment, the turbulent passions of living men. Well! she would go there: would not peace be found in that austere place, a silence which commanded piety, nay! a certain protection? She hobbled up the road to the churchyard, a deplorable, unwieldy figure, shivering, splashed by the rain-drops which had begun to fall. By the time she reached the path between the graves, the crowd (it was quite that, about forty men and women) came up with her, and fell to taunting her, reviling her, even cursing her, the wretch! as she stood white and shaking. Some women—the three girls who had passed her not an hour before were with them—drew near and laid violent, punishing hands on her. They pulled off her mean thin shawl, her stained bodice, her torn

torn, bedraggled skirts, and left her naked, save for a flimsy under garment, in the gathering darkness which would not come quickly to cover her, amid the raging villagers. A lump of mud struck her, and a stone which followed it cut open her cheek. When she saw that she was to be stoned out of her birth-place like a dog, she gasped a word ("Pardon" was it?) and started in a clumsy, uneven fashion to run. Heavily, blindly, she stumbled down the line of hooting rustics, till a flint hurled by a young man not yet twenty struck her between the shoulders, and brought her—the poor martyr!—to the ground at his feet. She managed to scramble to her knees, and looked into his face. When she recognized him, the father of her unborn child, all her grief, all her loathing of the one night spent in his company which had brought her to this degradation, all her scorn at finding him there, were vented in a great, bitter cry:

"Harry!"

He shoved her roughly, seizing her shoulders, and the people gave a shout of derision. She stretched out her arms towards the churchyard, as if imploring the indifferent dead—her own dead in particular—to take notice, to bear testimony; then broken, sobbing, she passed down the road gropingly, careless whether the stones hit her or fell short of her, till her form was wrapped in rain, and so lost to sight on the crest of the hill.

YIELD

(Propoundeth the Fruit of Seed)

IT was when the summer afternoon was most pleasant, about four o'clock, that a young man—a farm labourer with sun-browned face and brown toil-marked hands—rounded a corner of the road and came to a stand in the village street. It was delightful to pause, and rest there, with the bees murmuring softly, the trees waving, and the splash of a far-off stream just touching his ears. The stream's noise, after a while, the warble of it, its cool song, made him thirsty—some dust of the sunny lanes had got into his throat—and he moved slowly towards the "Nag's Head," his cap in his hand, letting the breeze soothe him, and the quietude of the peaceful neighbourhood. He entered the inn, nodding freely, with a large smile which shewed his white teeth, at the three or four rustics who were seated in the tap-room drinking mugs of ale, talking heavily with slow words; then when he was comfortable, placed in a corner, a mug of ale before him too, he joined in the talk. Yes, he had come from a distance: he "belonged" actually to a town some leagues away, but he had been

been working in the fields during the summer, passing from farm to farm, hardly knowing where he would be the next week. The season had been so bad: even to-day, fine as it was, had a certain film in the atmosphere, a torpor which boded more rain. The others grew confidential: they liked this young fellow who had somewhat the flavour of an adventurer, a toiler in perilous unknown places; and a farmer's trap drawn by a brown cob, which, in good time, drove up to the door, hardly damped a familiar conversation. The farmer alighted, leaving a pretty, youthful woman in the trap—his wife, he called her to the landlady with whom he entered the tap-room: a burly man, with a whip in his hand, about forty, wearing a low white felt hat, talking loudly, tossing easy salutations. He sat down at the table with the labourers, taking the strange labourer too into his favour, bestowing his patronage on him as on the rest. But for him, this strange labourer, the presence of the new-comer was gravely disturbing. He who felt kindly to all men, found himself, of a sudden, torn by an inexplicable hatred of this prosperous, amiable person. Surely he was crazed!—the sun with one of its thin penetrating darts had, in his long journey under it, struck him mad. His great loathing of this man he had never seen before—he felt too, in part, as one feels in a disturbed dream, that he had some wrong to avenge—his loathing and abomination

tion of the man was come quite suddenly, ere the farmer had even spoken. How was it that he felt himself, thickly yet tumultuously, to be in an open space—a churchyard perhaps—with the rain and darkness around, harried by an angry crowd, bruised by a stone flung by some one—by that one over there! How was it? This corner—was it not too hot? Yes, that was it—he would move—soon. Well? No! No! he must not! The picture on the wall over there—it was so curious, so interesting—why was it upside down? Why was it—and then with a shout he had sprung into the middle of the room and seized the farmer by the throat.

The woman in the trap outside, hearing a tumult, leaped to the ground and rushed in. What she saw was the farmer with a man at his feet whom he was lashing unmercifully with his driving-whip —lashing brutally, as though he would beat him to death—and the others standing open-mouthed, frightened, gazing.

"Harry!" she cried.

Her cry seemed to pierce the head of the man on the floor—he had been so gay that morning!— seemed to cut his head in two. Clumsily he got to his feet and stood staring idiotically at the company, rolling vacant, senseless eyes, not wiping the blood from his face. Then he went back to his corner happily, and sat down there, and began to play childishly with the mugs on the table.

VAUNT

VAUNT

IT will be seen from what I have said in other pages, that men's professions are empty things, and not at all to be trusted if they are not endorsed with corresponding actions. This is not as it should be, or as moralists would wish; but I draw my conclusions rather from things as they are, than from things as they should be. It is a supreme ruse of men to persuade themselves that they are virtuous and honourable, and to applaud any one who tells them so. And as you will see men admire in others just those qualities which they themselves can by no means acquire, in like manner do men admire virtue and honour. Nay! they instinctively encourage these qualities, since they know that the truthful and honourable are generally an easy prey for the disingenuous.

Hence it follows that it is as idle to proclaim your virtues as your vices. For none believes you save the credulous; and to be credulous is come to mean in our day to be foolish. There be some who boast of a few vices so that they may gain a reputation for frankness; but the result is, that
men

men attribute to these boasters not only the vices which they profess, but many others to boot. So they are tripped by their own snare. 'Tis better to boast of your virtues, since by repetition and a loud mouth you may get a few to believe in them; but the most part of men will esteem you indecent and a hypocrite. If you must vaunt, the best vaunting, believe it, is that of the Pharisee. So you can in conversation (with more grace if you are sedulous to keep a holy mien for the outer world) while belittling your own attempts at virtue, rejoice that you are not so graceless as such a one, your neighbour. From this we get inversion of the adage, which makes a truth: that people who live in glass houses should always throw stones. Still, if you fall from this position of Pharisee, you will be more hurt than if you were openly vicious.

The finest wisdom is to speak in a mean, so that none can tell whether you be a saint or a scoundrel. Yet in this must the scales be held with an obsequious hand, sometimes inclining to vice and sometimes to virtue, as the need demands. For in every man whose vices are rebuked by your virtues you have an enemy; whereas, no man is offended by the thought that he is more virtuous than you: and indeed it is a good art to exalt a man's virtues in comparison with your own vices, if you wish to gain anything from him. On the other side, if you profess virtue men will more
readily

readily put their trust in you; and this not because they think your virtue genuine, but because they think that your protestations before the world must withhold you from the commission of any outrageous deed which, if discovered, would bring you to public shame. Yet, as I say, 'tis best to be taciturn concerning your virtue and vice, your nobility and valour; for it is a plain truth, and one well observed, that the man who is most froward in his arm-chair is the first to collapse if he be resolutely faced.

HAVE

HAVE

A MAN with only a ragged coat to his back can be as great as a rich noble, if he never permit the rich noble to oblige him, or shew that he is awed by the other's magnificence. For who can think himself greater than you, when he finds that he has only what you do not want? Therein lies the point of the oft-told story of Diogenes and Alexander. But in this I would not be understood to speak of the favours of kings, which a man may accept respectably, since he is one of the people by whose favour the king rules; or of the favours of republics, which are constructed and held together by the people. Rather do I aim at those who incline to the servile before private fortune greater than their own. The average man pours incense from his eyes. You shall see a crowd gaping at a coach and four, so that the owner of the equipage thinks: How wonderful I am, since the world stands a-gaze at my passing! Men and women will hang about the doors of a house where there is a rout, so that they may see the ladies, who often are but vain painted dolls, pass to their carriages.

Others

Others will scheme and wriggle, and bear snubs and flouts, to get a card for that very rout; for thus they excite the delicious stares of the envious. Others, again, flock to some park or picture-gallery which the owner has disdainfully thrown open: and while they wander in hushed admiration, the proprietor puffs his cheeks and thinks of his condescension in making his property, for a few hours, free to the rabble. I had rather never see the finest picture in the world than see it in a private gallery in this fashion which reeks of the backstairs. I refuse to drop incense into any man's censer which he keeps smoking under his nose. A good rule is, never to put your foot in a place whence any man or woman can expel you at pleasure. 'Tis better to exclude than to be extruded. If you really contemn, you cannot be contemned; for it is in the power of any man, however humble and solitary, to say of the rest of mankind in the words of the poet: *Odi profanum vulgus et arceo.*

But here I would prevent you from concluding that I deliver any message of contentment. To despise what you can by no means have, is not opposed to grasping what you are able by force or stratagem. You are not to be contented with your lot unless you are at a height; and a man satisfied with lowliness (unless he be striving to be canonized, when he has a high object in view) is a sorry sight. Napoleon, when he was only general of the army of Italy,

Italy, was one day discussing affairs of state with certain envoys in a chamber in which there was a throne; and to the amazement of the others, he sprang up the steps and seated himself upon the throne, so that nothing in the room could be higher than himself. And let none say that I quote this great man too often; for he is the perfect modern example of an astonishing career, which he directed by unrelenting egoism, arts and wiles, and a low esteem of his fellow men. Rather than wander through life a colourless nonentity, be angry, and sin not, or sin, whichever you can do best. If you cannot be possessed by God, get yourself possessed by the devil. A thief, if he be successful in his thieving, may come to kneel in church a respected burgher. Strive to get wings for an ascension from the flat average. However you arrive at an end—arrive: or die struggling, not flabby. Dare all things rather than

> "Live a coward in thine own esteem,
> Letting I dare not wait upon I would."

BOW

BOW

A LOW man thinks, that by being rude he shews his independence. Certainly you shall often find boors, and what we now call "self-made men," turbulent and outrageous towards their inferiors, and insolent to their betters. Hence it has been well observed, that the worst master is he who has been himself a servant. A boor reasons that by raising his cap he lowers himself; and a vulgar rich man dreams fondly that arrogance implies importance.

But, on the other side, almost as grave a fault is condescension. Some are weak enough to imagine that those below them in station are pleased and awed by a few words spoken from a height. So far is this from the truth, that it may be laid down as a rule, that the man to whom you condescend becomes your enemy. Before you turn patron, it were well to be sure that you are in a posture to patronize. It is a great mistake to be mistaken about yourself. If you be not very great, or if he want nothing from you, the man to whom you obviously unbend must consider you impertinent. Moreover, he he may be laughing at you; and what a sting is there for your dignity! If you take thought to condescend to some inferior, it is a first necessity to purge your manner of condescension; for condescension is an art, and the highest art (as the maxim runs) is the concealment of art. Bacon writes of Julius Cæsar: "As he was the greatest "master of dissimulation, there was not a relick of "his nature left, but what art had improved; yet no- "thing of artifice, nothing of affectation appeared." A crafty man who exposes his wiles, loses what he most needs: confidence. In likewise, he who condescends, calls up what he least expects: enmity. It is best to turn the same face to a fellow as to a prince, save at times when it is advantageous to be haughty and insolent. It is good wisdom, if you are talking with some one in great place, and a mean man (yet one whose friendship may further you) happens to pass, to break off your conversation with a hasty word, and address yourself pleasantly and without concern to the passenger. So you make his friendship solid; for he thinks you must esteem him since you desert presently your fine friend for his company: and you may also be well with the potentate, for he may praise your urbanity and kindness of heart. But if you bring any condescension into this, it were better not to have spoken.

Cunning and over-subtile men most often fall to the other extreme, and shew themselves humble and
obsequious.

obsequious. This manner, if put on with an inferior, breeds distrust; and to one of greater station or power it reveals the sycophant. And because sycophants are like fawning animals that may bite, it will not be amiss to note some of their tricks.

Most sycophants will laugh boisterously at your feeble humour, and look low when you are sullen. The common sycophant finds out some quality wherein you excel, and plays his tune on that string. The gross praise you for qualities which you know you have not. Others, more astute, discover some merit which you envy in another, and while denying it to him, attribute it to you; for men take the dose with less misgiving in this way. Still, there be some who revolt at too open flattery; so your careful sycophant will ascertain the content of his vessel that he may know when to stop pumping. But such a revolt is little to be feared; for a man who takes flattery is like a man who takes morphia, till it comes to pass that he is miserable without it. If your sycophant has an enemy whom you can crush, he will strike at him through you by filling your mind with lies and tales, and relating how the enemy despises you on your nicest point: nay, he will even take the part of his enemy the better to rouse you to anger. Many sycophants have thus brought their patrons to the ground. A poisonous sycophant is he who affects a blunt and harsh manner, smiling but glumly at his patron's jests,

jests, and offering a shew of independence in discourse. This he does that the patron may exclaim: "Behold an honest man amongst a crowd "of flatterers!" But this game is dangerous: for by pushing too far he may get a kick from his patron's boot; like a dog which is esteemed a good watcher, but nevertheless, if his barking becomes troublesome, is presently despatched. So it was with Junius Gallio, who made a proposition to Tiberius by which he thought to shew his care for the army, and at the same time compass a flattery, and of whom Tacitus writes: *Hoc pretium Gallio meditatæ adulationis tulit, statim curia, deinde Italia exactus.* To conclude, all sycophants will desert you the moment they find one who can more readily further their ends; so they are of no more advantage to the private fortune, than hired foreign soldiers to a state.

Nothing in life is worth crawling for. To conciliate is hard enough; but in that there is often gain. On the other hand, a sycophant has nothing in the end but gibes and spits. For the patron holds the sycophant in contempt even while he is using him: and when the sycophant's value is past, as his patron has not the least respect for him, he is thrown aside like a worn shoe.

WILL

WILL

I

HAVE the dead still power after they are laid in the earth? Do they rule us, by the power of the dead, from their awful thrones? Do their closed eyes become menacing beacons, and their paralyzed hands reach out to scourge our feet into the paths which they have marked out? Ah, surely when the dead are given to the dust, their power crumbles into the dust!

Often during the long summer afternoons, as they sat together in a deep window looking out at the Park of the Sombre Fountains, he thought of these things. For it was at the hour of sundown, when the gloomy house was splashed with crimson, that he most hated his wife. They had been together for some months now; and their days were always spent in the same manner—seated in the window of a great room with dark oak furniture, heavy tapestry, and rich purple hangings, in which a curious decaying scent of lavender ever lingered. For an hour at a time he would stare at her intensely as she sat before him—tall, and pale, and fragile,

fragile, with her raven hair sweeping about her neck, and her languid hands turning over the leaves of an illuminated missal—and then he would look once more at the Park of the Sombre Fountains, where the river lay, like a silver dream, at the end. At sunset the river became for him turbulent and boding—a pool of blood; and the trees, clad in scarlet, brandished flaming swords. For long days they sat in that room, always silent, watching the shadows turn from steel to crimson, from crimson to gray, from gray to black. If by rare chance they wandered abroad, and moved beyond the gates of the Park of the Sombre Fountains, he might hear one passenger say to another, "How beautiful she is!" And then his hatred of his wife increased a hundredfold.

So he was poisoning her surely and lingeringly—with a poison more wily and subtle than that of Cæsar Borgia's ring—with a poison distilled in his eyes. He was drawing out her life as he gazed at her; draining her veins, grudging the beats of her heart. He felt no need of the slow poisons which wither the flesh, of the dread poisons which set fire to the brain; for his hate was a poison which he poured over her white body, till it would no longer have the strength to hold back the escaping soul. With exultation he watched her growing weaker and weaker as the summer glided by: not a day, not an hour passed that she did not pay toll
to

to his eyes: and when in the autumn there came upon her two long faints which resembled catalepsy, he fortified his will to hate, for he felt that the end was at hand.

At length one evening, when the sky was gray in a winter sunset, she lay on a couch in the dark room, and he knew she was dying. The doctors had gone away with death on their lips, and they were left, for the moment, alone. Then she called him to her side from the deep window where he was seated looking out over the Park of the Sombre Fountains.

"You have your will," she said. "I am dying."

"My will?" he murmured, waving his hands.

"Hush!" she moaned. "Do you think I do not know? For days and months I have felt you drawing the life of my body into your life, that you might spill my soul on the ground. For days and months as I have sat with you, as I have walked by your side, you have seen me imploring pity. But you relented not, and you have your will; for I am going down to death. You have your will, and my body is dead; but my soul cannot die. No!" she cried, raising herself a little on the pillows: "my soul shall not die, but live, and sway an all-touching sceptre lighted at the stars."

"My wife!"

"You have thought to live without me, but you will never be without me. Through long nights when

when the moon is hid, through dreary days when the sun is dulled, I shall be at your side. In the deepest chaos illumined by lightning, on the loftiest mountain-top, do not seek to escape me. You are my bond-man: for this is the compact I have made with the Cardinals of Death."

At the noon of night she died; and two days later they carried her to a burying-place set about a ruined abbey, and there they laid her in the grave. When he had seen her buried, he left the Park of the Sombre Fountains and travelled to distant lands. He penetrated the most unknown and difficult countries; he lived for months amid Arctic seas; he took part in tragic and barbarous scenes. He used himself to sights of cruelty and terror: to the anguish of women and children, to the agony and fear of men. And when he returned after years of adventure, he went to live in a house the windows of which overlooked the ruined abbey and the grave of his wife, even as the window where they had erewhile sat together overlooked the Park of the Sombre Fountains.

And here he spent dreaming days and sleepless nights—nights painted with monstrous and tumultuous pictures, and moved by waking dreams. Phantoms haggard and ghastly swept before him; ruined cities covered with a cold light edified themselves in his room; while in his ears resounded the trample of retreating and advancing armies, the clangour

clangour of squadrons, and noise of breaking war. He was haunted by women who prayed him to have mercy, stretching out beseeching hands— always women—and sometimes they were dead. And when the day came at last, and his tired eyes reverted to the lonely grave, he would soothe himself with some eastern drug, and let the hours slumber by as he fell into long reveries, murmuring at times to himself the rich, sonorous, lulling cadences of the poems in prose of Baudelaire, or dim meditative phrases, laden with the mysteries of the inner rooms of life and death, from the pages of Sir Thomas Browne.

On a night, which was the last of the moon, he heard a singular scraping noise at his window, and upon throwing open the casement he smelt the heavy odour which clings to vaults and catacombs where the dead are entombed. Then he saw that a beetle—a beetle, enormous and unreal—had crept up the wall of his house from the graveyard, and was now crawling across the floor of his room. With marvellous swiftness it climbed on a table placed near a couch on which he was used to lie, and as he approached, shuddering with loathing and disgust, he perceived to his horror that it had two red eyes like spots of blood. Sick with hatred of the thing as he was, those eyes fascinated him— held him like teeth. That night his other visions left him, but the beetle never let him go—nay!
compelled

compelled him, as he sat weeping and helpless, to study its hideous conformation, to dwell upon its fangs, to ponder on its food. All through the night that was like a century—all through the pulsing hours—did he sit oppressed with horror gazing at that unutterable, slimy vermin. At the first streak of dawn it glided away, leaving in its trail the same smell of the charnel-house; but to him the day brought no rest, for his dreams were haunted by the abominable thing. All day in his ears a music sounded—a music thronged with passion and wailing of defeat, funereal and full of great alarums; all day he felt that he was engaged in a conflict with one in armour, while he himself was unharnessed and defenceless—all day, till the dark night came, when he observed the abhorred monster crawling slowly from the ruined abbey, and the calm, neglected Golgotha which lay there in his sight. Calm outwardly; but beneath perhaps—how disturbed, how swept by tempest! With trepidation, with a feeling of inexpiable guilt, he awaited the worm—the messenger of the dead. And this night and day were the type of nights and days to come. From the night of the new moon, indeed, till the night when it began to wane, the beetle remained in the grave; but so awful was the relief of those hours, the transition so poignant, that he could do nothing but shudder in a depression as of madness. And his circumstances
were

were not merely those of physical horror and disgust: clouds of spiritual fear enveloped him: he felt that this abortion, this unspeakable visitor, was really an agent that claimed his life, and the flesh fell from his bones. So did he pass each day looking forward with anguish to the night; and then, at length, came the distorted night full of overwhelming anxiety and pain.

II

AT dawn, when the dew was still heavy on the grass, he would go forth into the graveyard and stand before the iron gates of the vault in which his wife was laid. And as he stood there, repeating wild litanies of supplication, he would cast into the vault things of priceless value: skins of man-eating tigers and of leopards; skins of beasts that drank from the Ganges, and of beasts that wallowed in the mud of the Nile; gems that were the ornament of the Pharaohs; tusks of elephants, and corals that men had given their lives to obtain. Then holding up his arms, in a voice that raged against heaven he would cry: "Take these, O avenging soul, and leave me in quiet! Are not these enough?"

And after some weeks he came to the vault again bringing with him a consecrated chalice studded with jewels which had been used by a priest at Mass, and a ciborium of the purest gold. These he filled with the rare wine of a lost vintage, and placing them within the vault he called in a voice of storm: "Take these, O implacable soul, and spare thy bond-man! Are not these enough?"

And last he brought with him the bracelets of the woman he loved, whose heart he had broken by parting with her to propitiate the dead. He brought

brought a long strand of her hair, and a handkerchief damp with her tears. And the vault was filled with the misery of his heart-quaking whisper: "O my wife, are not *these* enough?"

But it became plain to those who were about him that he had come to the end of his life. His hatred of death, his fear of its unyielding caress, gave him strength; and he seemed to be resisting with his thin hands some palpable assailant. Plainer and more deeply coloured than the visions of delirium, he saw the company which advanced to combat him: in the strongest light he contemplated the scenery which surrounds the portals of dissolution. And at the supreme moment, it was with a struggle far greater than that of the miser who is forcibly parted from his gold, with an anguish far more intense than that of the lover who is torn from his mistress, that he gave up his soul.

On a shrewd, gray evening in the autumn they carried him down to bury him in the vault by the side of his wife. This he had desired; for he thought that in no other vault however dark, would the darkness be quite still; in no other resting-place would he be allowed to repose. As they carried him they intoned a majestic threnody—a chaunt which had the deep tramp and surge of a triumphant march, which rode on the winds, and sobbed through the boughs of ancient trees. And having come to the vault they gave him to the grave, and knelt

knelt on the ground to pray for the ease of his spirit. *Requiem æternam dona ei, Domine!*

But as they prepared to leave the precincts of the ruined abbey, a dialogue began within the vault—a dialogue so wonderful, so terrible, in its nature, its cause, that as they hearkened they gazed at one another in the twilight with wry and pallid faces.

And first a woman's voice.

"You are come."

"Yes, I am come," said the voice of a man. "I yield myself to you—the conqueror."

"Long have I awaited you," said the woman's voice. "For years I have lain here while the rain soaked through the stones, and snow was heavy on my breast. For years while the sun danced over the earth, and the moon smiled her mellow smile upon gardens and pleasant things. I have lain here in the company of the worm, and I have leagued with the worm. You did nothing but what I willed; you were the toy of my dead hands. Ah, you stole my body from me, but I have stolen your soul from you!"

"And is there peace for me—now—at the last?"

The woman's voice became louder, and rang through the vault like a proclaiming trumpet. "Peace is not mine! You and I are at last together in the city of one who queens it over a mighty

mighty empire. Now shall we tremble before the queen of Death."

The watchers flung aside the gates of the vault and struck open two coffins. In a mouldy coffin they found the body of a woman having the countenance and warmth of one who has just died. But the body of the man was corrupt and most horrid, like a corpse that has lain for years in a place of graves.

OWE

OWE

MUCH has been said of the respect due from children to parents, and too little of the respect due from parents to children. Parents owe the same reparation to their children that one man owes to another whom he has led within an infected house. For the world is a house full of vile humours and disorders, into which men and women have been dragged without their consent: and, sure, few would arrive if they had the chances put fairly before them.

Some parents are wicked and perverse enough to believe that they have conferred such a benefit on a child by giving it life, that their duty really ends there, and that all else they do for the child is by way of favour. They even have the effrontery to look for thanks. Yet who is thankful to one that has made him miserable? For consider: life is so heavy, that although a horror of death is natural to man, men kill themselves every day to escape the burthen. Even princes, and those born to high place and outward happiness, have their hours and years of grinding misery; and there are

are cases of princes who have come to suicide.
The diseases of parents are often increased in the
children a hundredfold; and the delicate nervous
tremours of a mother may make her child a wretched
outcast. A hopeless man is the sin of his parents,
and workhouses are built by such sins. No;
children need not thank their rich parents for sending them to a university, or their poor parents for
setting them to a trade. These things do not
atone for calling one out of nothingness to the
griefs and anxieties of existence, and the terror of
oncoming death which grips all who live long
enough to think. And let no parent puff his
cheeks and say of his child: Let him work as I have
done! for he has no warrant from the universe to
create a child deliberately, and then order it to
work. If you be looking for immorality, in an
action like that you have an example at your hand.
A child who inherits riches from his parents, need
only recognize that they were not quite knaves
enough to add poverty to his other troubles. A
parent who is not satisfied with his child, by the
very fact acknowledges his mistake. In any case,
the child can reflect that he came to his parents by
their own wish, and that they are in the position
of forcing their company upon him. Can you
wonder that children are sometimes bored by
their parents?

If you believe in a benign God, you insult Him
by

by saying that He is responsible for the entrance of all children into the world. How could a kind God give to a drunken brute with a starving wife and ten children, an eleventh? Rather (if your God represent your good deeds, and the devil your bad deeds) let the matter rest with the devil, and let him be credited with the crime of dragging the wretched creature in sin and ignominy through this world, to prepare it for even fiercer tortures in the next.

It is unreasonable for a father to expect his son to be a man like himself, or for a mother to be irritated because she cannot discover her own traits in her daughter; and this because the son and daughter have the mixed blood of their father and mother, and this mixture must produce characters different from either.

Parents who would gain the love of a child must treat it as they would one to whom they have done some great wrong of which they have repented. They will also do well to give the child something to admire in them; for no child can love a parent who is tyrannical, capricious, or worthless. Most parents take the affection of their children for granted, as though the words *Father* and *Mother* were love-potions; and some even foolishly order their children to love them, as though anybody could summon love by a command. But what Machiavel says of men in general, that they commonly

monly deceive themselves in respect of the love which they imagine others bear them, may be repeated with much force of parents and children. And even if a child come to love his parents without hypocrisy, they cannot be sure that he will not at some time reproach them. For a man must be very happy and fortunate in his life that a day does not come when he repents that he was ever born: and how can his mouth be full of blessings for his parents at the same time that he is cursing the hour of his birth? Further, children are not to be accounted unnatural if when their interests clash with those of their parents, they refuse to yield to their parents. The created has not the same affection for the creator, as the maker has for the thing he has made: hence when it comes to a conflict the child will suppress the parent. From the many examples of this upon record, I may cite what Tacitus relates ("Annals," lib. i., cap. 14) of Tiberius and his mother Livia, that the former, anxious lest his own grandeur should diminish as his mother's increased, would not appoint to her so much as a single Lictor, and prohibited any honours which the Senate was for paying her.

GLIDE

GLIDE

IN a hot dark room with a high ceiling three persons were sitting at a table: an old man, a woman with the pinched vindictive face of one who has ceded her virginity neither to God nor man, and a second man. Two guttering brown candles in silver candlesticks were set in the middle of the table. The second man was talking loudly and boastfully of the fine thing he intended to make of his life; he even saw his hands grasping a throne. The woman listened glumly, and the old man with a strange doubtful smile. At last, when the second man declared that he would be Bonaparte rather than Monk:

"You will be neither," said the woman. "You are too old."

He started in anger and surprise. "How can you say that I am too old, when I have not yet lived twenty-three years?"

"Nay!" replied the woman calmly. "Yesterday you had lived for fifty years."

At that he hid his face in his arms on the table. There fell a long silence, disturbed only by the ticking

ticking of the little spiders in the wood-work and the buzz of a fly that wandered round the lights. The old man gazed at the woman with heavy, care-worn looks. And the woman, she too gazed at the old man with a mean, subtile smile. As for the second man, his heart was mighty cold with the feeling that his life was over, when he had thought that it was just beginning. Buzz! buzz! Yes, it was age, weak and confused age, that was speaking in the fly's wings. After some hours he raised his head and darted a poisonous look at the old man.

"It is you who have done this!" he cried furiously. "You tied me to yourself and never let me know that I was growing old. You saw the years running through my fingers like dust, and you never told me to close my hand. Had you no fear of the curse, gray robber?"

"Alas! I was indeed afraid," said the old man sadly. "But I wished to keep you near me, for your lusty hardihood was like fresh music, and your plans made the blood sing in my shrivelled body."

The other let his head fall again on the table and sobbed. Then the old man got up and put his arm round the shoulders and gently stroked the thin whitening hair of the other. "Forget what is gone, forget what is gone," he murmured. "Let us go elsewhere. You still have life." But the other only shook with hard clinging sobs.

Thereupon

Thereupon the old man looked at the woman and frowned. "Why did you tell him?" he asked.

"What difference does it make?" she answered lightly. "He was always too young, and now he is too old."

SAID

SAID

FAME is an indolent jade that hangs about the market-cross talking loud emptiness, like a drum. Certainly, there can be no wisdom in a mouth full of rumours, nor can anything of import be gleaned from it. Wherefore Tertullian commenting on Virgil's line, *Fama malum, quo non aliud velocius ullum*, "Why does he call Fame an "ill?" he asks. "Because of her swiftness? Or "because she is an informer? Or because she is "a common liar? For the last reason, without "question." Hence it is good, if you hear any rumour bruited abroad concerning a man, to trace it back to the man's self, when you will usually find that it is false. For he has either set it in motion, or he has not; and in the last case the rumour is proved a lie without more ado. As for the first, there are men whose use is to let fall words which they would have believed, knowing that they will swell when they pass into common fame: as a ball, when it is rolled over and over in the mud, grows to twice its size. Yet this they do carelessly, and, as it were, in jest; so
that

that if they chance to be confronted with the rumour in its swelled state, they can reply: "This "I never said."

Popularity is rumour brought to its highest power. The populace cannot see for itself; and if it hear a few prating about their "geniuses," it will catch up the cry with a will. Not many men of real worth have presently gained the popular approval: and this is true even of those who have led the populace by the nose. I would cite the case of Napoleon, "a natural terror and "horror to all Phantasms," whose fortunes were low and desperate before Vendémiaire; and the case of Disraeli will be ready in your mind. These two, however, were popular in spite of the populace.

Whatever is new is in a measure startling; and men are stiff for usage and suspicious of novelty. It would seem to be wise, if you seek immediate popularity, to act as the people itself would act; yet so to daub and cast a glamour over your actions, that you appear to be directing and above the people. The most popular statesman, as has been not infrequently proved, is he in whom the manners and tastes of the average man are developed till they become a force. Thereupon the people sets this image of itself on high, deeming the image something great, and not perceiving that it is but worshipping itself: even as men adore a God to whom they attribute all their own passions
of

of hate and love, cruelty and vengeance. Likewise, it would seem that the popular writer must have a strictly conventional mind, so that he can write what the people feels, but is unable to express. Some of us have experienced an emotion of delight at hearing a familiar strain of music played in an unfamiliar place: so it is with the populace when it finds its own ideas in a book. That the goatherd who plays the familiar strain on his pipe is a great musician, I am not prepared to admit; but he may certainly consider himself so if he like, and no doubt there are many who think he is. I once read that a beautiful book called "Marius the "Epicurean" was "a failure with the public," whereat I fell to laughing; for I was unable to think that a man who could write such a book would have the public in his mind at all.

It is a good point, if you would be popular, not to stay too long in the company of one set of persons to the exclusion of others; for men with whom you commonly consort may (if you be garrulous) find out the limits of your mind and set evil rumours flying. Some reflection like this may be at the root of the saying of Jesus: "A prophet is "not without honour, but in his own country, and "among his own kin, and in his own house." Certainly, the most dire blows have often been aimed at men from clubs and other places, where they thought themselves most secure and at ease.

Further,

Further, before aiming at popularity you would do well to call to mind that no one can, with any reason, confidently hope to hold the favour of the people through a long life, however he may twist and accommodate himself; and that those who have been most popular, have not seldom declared, when by accident they were brought to the ground, that they were glad the struggle was over. And when all is said, a popular man has but a sorry life of starts, and fears, and surprises: he is like to one who holds the pulse of another whom he loves, who lies sick of a tidal fever.

LIFE is the opposite of death and objects to it; life is weaker than death and protests against it: yet it cannot be said that it is harder to die than to live, or that we struggle to live rather than not to die. Nor is it too curious to think, that life is a rebellion against nature: for the forces of nature are against life; many live but a brief span, and cannot live at all without long intervals of sleep; whereas, on the other side, everything dies, and that with the help and good will of nature. It is the instinct of men to fear death as the supreme evil: but this instinct is fitter for the animals with whom it is shared than for men, who can overcome instinct by reason. Even those who hold the ugly and material faith, that God has prepared a furnace in which it is ordained that they shall burn, need not, on that account, go in awe of death; for the spirit may be better tempered to suffering than the body. But if death be only the quenching of life, a most sound sleep: what then? We perceive, that all who are troubled, and anxious, and perplexed, look eagerly to sleep; and those to
whom

whom sleep comes not quickly, are fain to summon it by dormitive draughts. You have perhaps felt, when you have slept upon a sorry night, the horror and regret of waking to the morning's anguish. Have you not then wished that you might sleep indefinitely, or indeed that you might never wake? And yet sleep is a voluntary abdication of life: for a certain number of hours you agree to lie dead to the world. Sir Thomas Browne says: "We term "sleep a death; and yet it is waking that kills us, "and destroys those spirits that are the house of "life." Might not the dead repine if they were called back to life, and wonder what charm life had that they cherished it while they yet lived? Nay! those who have been brought near to death by sickness, are most often neither glad nor sorry that they have not died.

Wherefore, then, if death be a profound and lasting sleep, do men seek to avoid death, while they court and wait upon sleep? Because it is a lasting sleep? Yet life is not so pleasant but that men oft-times seek to forget it in a drugged and drunken somnolence, from which they hate to be aroused. Or because it is unknown? But year by year men venture into countries and on seas of which they have no chart or report; and the rich man who has never felt the bite of poverty, and who suddenly loses his money, of two unknowns not seldom prefers death. And we see that the
burthen

burthen of life is frequently more oppressive than the thought of death; for men turn to death from a very disgust and weariness of living. With this in his mind, the great modern poet majestically sings:

> "O Mort, vieux capitaine, il est temps! levons l'ancre!
> Ce pays nous ennuie, ô Mort! Appareillons!
> Si le ciel et la mer sont noirs comme de l'encre,
> Nos cœurs que tu connais sont remplis de rayons!"

Again, Tacitus relates of Lucius Arruntius, that being impeached, he resolved to die; and to the protests of his friends he answered that he had lived long enough: *Sibi satis ætatis, neque aliud paenitendum quam quod inter ludibria et pericula anxiam senectam toleravisset.* Saying these words, he opened his veins. From all this I conclude that death is not in itself an evil and a pain, but is made so by the accompaniments and trappings of death. Death-bed prayers, and weeping friends, and coffins and shrouds, and undertaker's men, lend a terror to what is not terrible, to what may even be sweet. If a man could lie down and die in the open with the wind about his face; if he had no vault to dread or graveyard mould—yea! if he could take to his bed to die, as he would to sleep, quietly, without the clamour of on-lookers; I can conceive that he would turn from life to death with the eagerness of a lover seeking his mistress. I would hazard that the last gaspings are no more than a great and overpowering drowsiness; for I have

have seen men whose terror of death while they were in strength was painful and almost mean, at the last hour die peacefully, even gladly, with dream-like smiles. It is very observable, that athletes, and other men of a healthy and full habit of body, have a greater fear of death than the sick and pining, who may be supposed to have a close and intimate view of it.

You will take me as speaking of death itself, and not of the roads to death, which are often tortuous and full of agony, but which are really a part of life. Of these roads, surely one of the most grievous is that of the condemned murderer, with whom a term of days must elapse betwixt his sentence and his taking off. For (if he be not brutishly devoid of sense) he is tormented with disgrace, regrets, and apprehensions to such a degree, that there is hardly a man educated in civility who, if he were so unhappily placed as to have to choose, without any glance at the ethical aspect of the question, whether to be a murderer, or as a murderer's victim to be suddenly blotted out, would not select, without hesitation, the part of the victim. I write here of murders springing from private passions; and not of murders by fanatics who are upheld by their cause, or of murders perpetrated to seat princes more securely on their thrones. Of this last kind was the fusillading of the Duc d'Enghien in a trench at Vincennes,

cennes, by order of Napoleon: which some indeed have denounced as a foul and glaring murder; but of which Hazlitt more wisely declared, that if he were in Napoleon's place, and the thing had to be done over again, he would act like Napoleon.

I know of nothing more inspiring, or which proves, in a more consoling way that death is not an evil, but rather a good, than what is related in Plato's Apology of Socrates. There it is set forth, that Socrates, addressing his judges just before he was despatched, said to them, that it was very strange that the prophetic voice of his demon (or familiar spirit) which never failed before of dissuading him in matters of the smallest moment, where the consequence would be ill, should at that hour, in the worst of evils, according to the opinion of his judges, be silent: "For it could not be" (says Socrates) "but that I should hear his usual dissuasive was I "not upon doing that which would turn to my ad-"vantage." And so, being convinced that death is a natural rest, and not cruel and outrageous, I do not find myself in tune with those who while they dread not the actual throes of dissolution, are yet perturbed that the world shall go on after they decease, and gaze on cathedrals and such lasting monuments with eyes full of self-pity. Still, their existence was not contemplated by the builders when the cathedral was edified, who built to please themselves; nor were the builders, in their turn, considered
when

when in some later century another arch was added, or another buttress reared. Man acts as he wills in his own time; and every generation has the same power. If men had rivals like Methuselah, then indeed they might well be in pain; but as it is, every man can reflect that no one who comes after him will have a much longer tenure of the world than he has himself.

It is wise, as all agree, to meditate upon death, as you would study a country into which you must one day travel; but it is not wise to dwell upon the chances of another world, about which you cannot possibly know anything certain, till you become a coward. Many are made unfit for this world by preparing themselves for the next. Neither is it wise, but most silly and futile, to dwell on the vulgar appendages of death, such as coffins and damp earthen graves, which have nothing to do with death, and are created by the barbarism of men, and with which when you are dead you can have no concern. For I am not of those who fear to be wrapped in a cloud of nothingness; and I do not esteem Cato the more because he convinced himself out of Plato as to the immortality of the soul ere he took his life. When I seek my bed, I had rather have a night of sound blank sleep, than a sleep confused and coloured by dreams.

Here I bring to an end the monologues to which you

you have lent an ear with such patient and courtly grace. Either you hate me because I have shewn you the bodkin truth so nakedly that the blood has tingled in your cheek; or you applaud me for not throwing over the figure of truth the gaudy veil of hypocrisy. However it may be, I keep in mind that you have listened, and I bear you no ill-will. Farewell!

THE END

CHISWICK PRESS:—CHARLES WHITTINGHAM AND CO.
TOOKS COURT, CHANCERY LANE, LONDON.

www.ingramcontent.com/pod-product-compliance
Lightning Source LLC
Chambersburg PA
CBHW031349160426
43196CB00007B/791